Published by Mz. Kim Productions
4263 Tierra Rejada Rd #151
Moorpark, CA 93021
www.mzkimproductions.com

ISBN: 978-1-962106-08-5

Printed in United States of America
First Printing: August 2023
Date of Copyright: July 5,2023
Cover design by Marina Trapanese
Illustrations by Marina Trapanese
Edited by Joshua Nickel

For permissions, please contact: Mz. Kim Productions
4263 Tierra Rejada Rd #151
Moorpark, CA 93021
www.mzkimproductions.com
mzkimproductions@gmail.com

The characters and events portrayed in this book are fictitious. Any similarity to real persons, living or dead, is purely coincidental and not intended by the author.

Dedication:

To my beloved family and friends,

This book is dedicated to all of you who have been a source of love, support, and inspiration in my life. You have been my pillars of strength, encouraging me to pursue my dreams and share my stories with the world.

To my grandma Margie who instilled in me a love for storytelling and a deep faith in God, thank you for nurturing my imagination and teaching me the importance of family bonds.

To my siblings, who have always been my biggest cheerleaders, thank you for believing in me and reminding me of my worth during moments of doubt.

To my dear friends, who have stood by my side through thick and thin, thank you for your unwavering support and for being my sounding board as I embarked on this writing journey.

To my own children, who have brought immeasurable joy and inspiration into my life, thank you for being my constant source of love and motivation. You are my greatest blessings.

And finally, to my precious grandchildren, Zipporah and Zion, this book is dedicated to you. May it serve as a reminder of the love and wisdom passed down through generations, and may it inspire you to always trust in God's power and believe in the miracles He can perform in your lives.

Thank you, my dear family and friends, for being my rock and for being a part of this beautiful journey. Your love and support mean the world to me.

With all my love,

Dr. K.T. Zulkowski

Author's Note:

Dear readers,

I am delighted to present to you "Grandma Margie's Tale: The Valley of Dry Bones." This book was inspired by the timeless story found in the book of Ezekiel in the Bible. As a writer, I believe in the power of storytelling to captivate young minds and teach valuable lessons.

In this book, we follow the loving and wise Grandma Margie as she shares the story of the Valley of Dry Bones with her grandchildren, Zipporah and Zion. Through Grandma Margie's guidance, the children learn about the incredible power of God to bring life to what seems dead and hopeless.

I hope this book not only entertains young readers but also sparks their curiosity about the Bible and its stories. The story of the Valley of Dry Bones is a reminder that God's love and power are always present in our lives, ready to perform miracles.

As you read this book with your children, I encourage you to engage in conversations about faith, hope, and the importance of trusting in God. May this story inspire young hearts to believe in the extraordinary and to seek God's guidance in their own lives.

Thank you for joining Grandma Margie, Zipporah, and Zion on this adventure. May it bring joy, inspiration, and a deeper understanding of God's love.

With warmest regards,

Dr. K.T. Zulkowski

Educational Value:

1. Biblical Story: The book introduces children to the story of the Valley of Dry Bones from the book of Ezekiel in the Bible, helping them become familiar with important biblical narratives.

2. Faith and Miracles: The story emphasizes the importance of faith and trust in God's power to perform miracles, teaching children that nothing is impossible with God.

3. Problem-Solving: The story encourages children to think about how God can bring life to seemingly hopeless situations, fostering problem-solving skills and a positive mindset.

4. Family Bonding: The book highlights the special bond between grandparents and grandchildren, promoting the value of spending time together and passing down wisdom through storytelling.

5. Prayer and Hope: The story encourages children to pray and seek God's guidance, teaching them the importance of hope and relying on God in challenging times.

Overall, "Grandma Margie's Tale: The Valley of Dry Bones" combines a captivating story, beautiful illustrations, and valuable life lessons to inspire children's faith and teach them about the power of God's miracles.

Grandma MarGie's tale:

The Valley of Dry Bones

Written by: Dr.K.T.Zulkowski

Illustrated by: Marina Trapanese

Grandma Margie:
Once upon a time, my dear Zipporah and Zion,
there was a fascinating story in the Bible that
I want to share with you today.
It's called "The Valley of Dry Bones."

Zion: Grandma, why are there bones in the valley?

Grandma Margie: Good question, Zion!
These bones belonged to people who had died a long time ago.
But God had a special plan for them.

Zipporah: Grandma, what does the Bible say about these bones?

Grandma Margie: Well, Zipporah, the Bible says that God took the prophet Ezekiel to this valley full of dry bones. God wanted to show Ezekiel something amazing!

Zion: Grandma, what did Ezekiel see?

Grandma Margie: Ezekiel saw that the bones were very dry, and there were so many of them. It seemed impossible for them to come back to life.

Zipporah: Grandma, what did God tell Ezekiel to do?

Grandma Margie: God told Ezekiel to speak to the bones and say, "Dry bones, hear the word of the Lord!"

Zion: Grandma, what happened next?

Grandma Margie: As Ezekiel spoke,
something incredible happened!
The bones started coming together, bone to bone,
and they formed complete skeletons.

Zipporah: Grandma, what happened after the skeletons formed?

Grandma Margie: Well, Zipporah, God made muscles and flesh cover the skeletons. They started to look like real people again!

Zion: Grandma, did the bodies come to life?

Grandma Margie: Yes, Zion! God breathed His breath into the bodies, and they came to life. They stood up, a great army of people!

Zion: Grandma, did the bodies come to life?

Grandma Margie: Yes, Zion! God breathed
His breath into the bodies, and they came to life.
They stood up, a great army of people!

Zipporah: Grandma, that's amazing! What does this story teach us?

*Grandma Margie: This story teaches us that with God,
nothing is impossible. He can bring life to what seems dead and hopeless.*

Zion: Grandma, can God do miracles like this today?

Grandma Margie: Absolutely, Zion! God is still in the business of performing miracles. He can bring life to our dreams, hopes, and even our relationships.

Zion: Grandma, can God do miracles like this today?

Grandma Margie: Absolutely, Zion! God is still in the business of performing miracles. He can bring life to our dreams, hopes, and even our relationships.

Zion: Grandma, thank you for sharing this incredible story with us!

Grandma Margie: You're welcome, my sweet grandchildren. Remember, God's love and power can bring life to any situation. Trust Him always!

Zipporah: Goodbye, Grandma Margie! We love you!

Grandma Margie: Goodbye, my precious ones! Remember, God is always with you, ready to perform miracles in your lives.

Zion: Grandma Margie's stories are always the best!

Zipporah: Yes, Zion. Let's remember the story of the Valley of Dry Bones and trust God to bring life to our dreams too!

www.ingramcontent.com/pod-product-compliance
Lightning Source LLC
Chambersburg PA
CBHW041527120626
46551CB00018B/2605